Insects and Creepy-Crawlies

Jinny Johnson

KINGFISHER
NEW YORK

KINGFISHER
LONDON & NEW YORK

Copyright © Kingfisher 2011
Published in the United States by Kingfisher,
175 Fifth Ave., New York, NY 10010
Kingfisher is an imprint of
Macmillan Children's Books, London.
All rights reserved.

Distributed in the U.S. by Macmillan,
175 Fifth Ave., New York, NY 10010

Illustrations by Peter Bull Art Studio

Library of Congress Cataloging-in-Publication data
has been applied for.

ISBN: 978-0-7534-6592-9

Kingfisher books are available for special promotions
and premiums. For details contact: Special Markets
Department, Macmillan, 175 Fifth Ave.,
New York, NY 10010.

For more information, please visit
www.kingfisherbooks.com

Printed in China
1 3 5 7 9 8 6 4 2
1TR/0411/WKT/UNTD/140MA

Picture credits

**The Publisher would like to thank the following
for permission to reproduce their material
(t = top, b = bottom, c = center, l = left, r = right):**

Page 4bl Shutterstock/Hordiena; 4cr Frank Lane Picture Agency
(FLPA)/Rene Krekels/Minden; 4–5b Photolibrary/John Warburton-Lee;
5tl Photoshot/Stephen Dalton/NHPA; 5tc Photoshot/Stephen Dalton/
NHPA; 5c Shutterstock/sad; 5tr Shutterstock/Vinicius Tupinam; 5cr
Shutterstock/Audrey Snider-Bell; 5br Photolibrary/Animals Animals; 6bl
Shutterstock/SF photo; 8cl Alamy/Laszlo Podor; 8c Photolibrary/Animals
Animals; 8br Alamy/Premaphotos; 9tl FLPA /Bjorn Van Lieshout/Minden;
9tr Naturepl/Warwick Sloss; 9c FLPA/Nigel Cattlin; 9bc Shutterstock/
Four Oaks; 9br FLPA/Bob Gibbons; 10bl FLPA/Scott Leslie/Minden;
12l FLPA/Malcolm Schuyl; 12tc Photolibrary/OSF; 12tr Ardea/Alan
Weaving; 12b Shutterstock/design56; 13tl Naturepl/Owen Newman;
13c Alamy/Graphic Science; 13tr FLPA/Fritz Polking; 13cl Science Photo
Library (SPL)/Bjorn Svensson; 13b Photolibrary/age footstock; 14tl
Ardea/Steve Downer; 16l FLPA/Ingo Arndt; 16br Naturepl/Andy Sands;
17tl Photolibrary/Garden Picture Library; 17tr Photolibrary/OSF; 17bl
Shutterstock/alle; 17br Naturepl/Kim Taylor; 18bl Naturepl/David Shale;
20t SPL/Kazuyoshi Nomachi; 20cl Alamy /Petra Wegner; 20c FLPA/
Matt Cole; 20cr FLPA/Konrad Wothe/Minden; 21tc Alamy/Nigel Cattlin;
21tr SPL/Norm Thomas; 21l FLPA/Bob Gibbons; 21br FLPA/ImageBroker/
Imagebroker; 22tl FLPA/Cisca Castelijns; 24tl FLPA/B Borrell Casals;
24c Naturepl/Kim Taylor; 25tl FLPA/Jef Meul/Minden; 25ctl Photolibrary/
Mauritius; 25tc Naturepl/Michael Durham; 25cr Photoshot /NHPA/John
Brackenbury; 25bl FLPA/Nigel Cattlin; 25br Photolibrary/Imagebroker;
26bl Naturepl/Robert Thompson; 28bl Ardea/Jean Paul Ferrero; 28br
Naturepl/Nick Garbutt; 29tl FLPA/Michael Quinton/Minden; 29ctl
Photolibrary/Imagebroker; 29tr Naturepl/Dave Bevan; 29cr FLPA/
ImageBroker/Imagebroker; 29b Photolibrary/OSF; 30tl Photolibrary/
Bios; 30tr Shutterstock/javarman; 30ctr Naturepl/Edwin Giesbers; 30cbl
Shutterstock/Kirsanov; 30cbr Shutterstock/Kirschner; 30bl Alamy/Mira;
30br Shutterstock/Marek R. Swadzba; 31tr Naturepl/Premaphotos;
31ctl Shutterstock/Alex_187; 31ctr Shutterstock/Peter Wey; 31cbr
Photoshot/Stephen Dalton/NHPA; 31br Photoshot/Daniel Heuclin/NHPA

Contents

More to explore

On some of the pages in this book, you will find colored buttons with symbols on them. There are four different colors, and each belongs to a different topic. Choose a topic, follow its colored buttons through the book, and you'll make some interesting discoveries of your own.

For example, on page 6 you'll find a red button, like this, next to a flower. The red buttons are about plants.

Page 23

Plants

There is a page number in the button. Turn to that page (page 23) to find a red button next to a flower in a meadow. Follow all the steps through the book, and at the end of your journey you'll find out how the steps are linked and discover even more information about this topic.

Creepy-crawlies and us

Record breakers   **Habitats**

The other topics in this book are creepy-crawlies and us, record breakers, and habitats. Follow the steps and see what you can discover!

World of creepy-crawlies

There are more types of insects on Earth than any other kind of creature. They live everywhere—except in the ocean—and eat almost every type of food. Besides insects, there are other creepy-crawlies such as snails, worms, and spiders.

grasshopper

feeler

leg

head

thorax

wing

abdomen

A grasshopper, like most insects, has six legs, two pairs of wings, and a pair of feelers, called antennae, on its head. Its body has three parts—the head, thorax, and abdomen.

Moths use their feelers to sense smells and tastes.

The male uses its big horns in battles with rival males.

At 2 in. (6cm) long, the **rhinoceros beetle** is one of the biggest of all beetles. It is one of the strongest insects, too, and can lift 850 times its own weight!

Most insects can **fly**, but other creepy-crawlies, such as spiders, cannot. Insects were the first creatures ever to take to the air—before birds and bats.

honeybees in flight

Flying insects do an important job, carrying pollen from flower to flower.

Earthworms have no legs but can tunnel underground.

Centipedes are not insects. These long-bodied creepy-crawlies live on land and scuttle around on their many legs—15 or more pairs! They are fierce hunters.

centipede

rhinoceros beetle

wolf spider

Spiders belong to a group of creepy-crawlies called arachnids. They have eight legs.

From egg to adult

Most insects start life as eggs. Some insect eggs hatch into tiny versions of their parents. Butterfly eggs hatch into wriggly caterpillars. Their job is to eat and grow as much as they can before turning into beautiful butterflies.

Page 23

What is this?

1. Fire ants are feasting on a monarch egg.

2. Eggs are laid one at a time and stuck to leaves.

3. A newly hatched caterpillar eats its egg.

? These are a caterpillar's stumpy little legs that allow it to crawl and climb.

Page 27

6

5

Monarch butterfly caterpillars are busy eating milkweed leaves and growing bigger and bigger. A full-grown caterpillar has made a hard outer case called a pupa or chrysalis. Inside this, the caterpillar is turning into a butterfly. Nearby, a butterfly has come out of its pupa and is ready to fly away.

 4 The caterpillar feeds on milkweed and grows bigger.

5 The caterpillar changes into a butterfly inside a pupa.

 6 Adult monarch butterflies fly and feed on nectar.

Starting life

Most insects and creepy-crawlies leave their eggs to hatch by themselves—their babies must start life on their own. But a few parents make sure their young have a good food supply when they hatch, and others even take care of their babies.

leftover nymph skin

scorpion babies on their mother's back

emperor scorpion

Scorpions are surprisingly caring mothers. The scorpion carries her tiny babies around on her back until they are big enough to take care of themselves.

A shield bug guards her young.

The young bugs have the same body shape as their parents.

damselfly

Housefly babies are legless maggots.

house fly

Damselfly
eggs hatch into
water-living creatures
called nymphs. When
a nymph is fully grown,
it crawls out of the water
up a plant stem. Its skin
splits and the adult
damselfly struggles
out, ready to
fly away.

Houseflies lay
eggs that hatch
into maggots. The
maggots feed and
grow and then turn
into adult flies.

Baby spiders, called spiderlings,
cluster together when they first
hatch. Then they spin small
silken threads that act like
kites to help them float
away to new homes.

Dung beetles collect dung
(animal poop) and roll it into
a neat ball. Then, the female
beetle lays her eggs in
the ball. When the eggs
hatch, the young
already have a meal—
of yummy dung!

ball
of dung

Insect nests

Honeybees make amazing nests. They live in large groups ruled by one female—the queen. The nest is made up of many small, six-sided cells, built with wax from the bees' bodies. Some cells contain eggs or young. Others store food.

Page 27

What is this?

1. Food cells are full of honey or pollen.

2. A bee baby, or larva, comes out of its cell.

3. The queen bee lays all of the eggs.

? This is a ball of pollen. The bee carries pollen in a special hair-lined area on each back leg.

There's always a lot to do in a bees' nest. Here, worker bees look after the eggs and young and keep the nest clean. Other workers gather pollen and nectar, a sweet liquid made by plants. Bees collect pollen to feed to their young and nectar for making honey to feed on in the winter. Can you see the queen in the center of the nest?

5

Page 22

Page 15

6

Page 22

Page 15

4 Worker bees do all of the work for the colony.

5 The sealed cells contain eggs or young.

6 A worker bee gathers pollen and nectar from a flower.

There are tiny spiderlings inside the nursery web.

weaver ants' nest

The nursery web spider carries her eggs with her while they develop. Just before they hatch, she spins a special nursery web and puts her eggs inside. The web keeps the young safe, but she also stays on guard nearby.

Weaver ants make their nests using living leaves on trees. A group of worker ants pulls the leaf edges together. Then, more workers stitch the edges using silk that they squeeze from their own young.

Making a nest

Many insects and creepy-crawlies are expert nest builders. Ants and termites live in big groups and make nests from soil, leaves, or pieces of wood. Some spiders protect their young with sheets of silk, while potter wasps make small mud nests for each of their babies.

Termites have soft bodies and cannot live out in the open for very long. They make nests on the ground or in trees to protect themselves. Ground nests can be 20 ft. (6m) high—that's taller than three people standing on top of one another.

ground nests

The towers are made of mud and termite spit. Most of the living quarters are underground.

tree nest

Tree nests are made from pieces of wood and termite spit. The termites also make small passageways on the branch or trunk for moving around under cover.

termite

Inside this pile of soil and pine needles is an ants' nest.

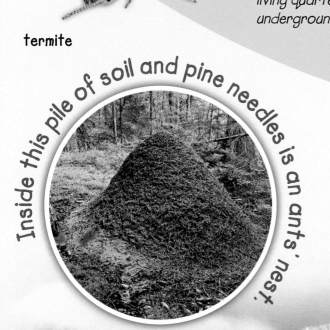

The potter wasp lays her egg in a pot-shaped mud nest. She then puts in some caterpillars and seals the nest. When the baby wasp hatches, it has a good supply of food.

The wasp paralyzes the caterpillars with her sting before she puts them in the nest.

What is this?

1 adult green darner dragonfly

2 The whirligig beetle uses its legs to paddle in circles.

3 The water boatman feeds on plants.

Page 30

Water creatures

Many insects and creepy-crawlies live in and around ponds, rivers, and streams. Some, such as dragonflies, start their lives in the water and then take to the air. Others spend their whole lives in the water and have legs shaped like small paddles for swimming.

On the stream bed, a fierce dragonfly nymph has just caught a young crayfish. Nearby, a giant water bug chases tadpoles. Water boatmen are not hunters. They feed on tiny water plants that they gather with their front legs. Whirligig beetles and water striders dart around the surface catching small prey.

Page 22

Page 30

4

5

6

These are a dragonfly nymph's strong jaws. The lower jaw shoots out to catch prey.

Life in the water

Most water-living insects and creepy-crawlies still need to breathe air. Some, such as the diving beetle, take air down from the surface. Others have breathing tubes like built-in snorkels. And the water spider makes its own diving bell.

breathing tube

front legs for grabbing prey

Before diving to catch prey, the **great diving beetle** collects bubbles of air under its wings. These allow it to breathe while underwater. The beetle swims well using its fringed back legs like oars.

great diving beetle

The water stick insect is a type of bug, not a stick insect. It hangs upside down from the water's surface and breathes through a tube at the end of its body as it watches for prey.

Water snails eat pondweed and other water plants.

A snail can hide away in its shell if it is in danger.

silvery diving bell filled with air

The water spider
is the only spider that spends its whole life in water. It makes a bell of silk, which it fills with air bubbles. When the spider catches prey, it takes the prey inside the bell to eat.

water spider

You can see an adult caddis fly on page 24 and an adult mosquito on page 25.

Mosquito larvae live and grow in water.

Caddis fly
eggs hatch into young (larvae) like little caterpillars. To protect its body, the larva makes a small outer case from leaves, twigs, and tiny stones, held together with silk.

caddis fly larva

Mini hunters

Many insects and creepy-crawlies are fierce predators, just like larger animals, and life can be dangerous on the jungle floor. These small hunters have weapons such as poisonous stings or sharp claws for attacking their prey.

What is this?

1. An assassin bug slurps up its prey.

2. The scorpion uses its sting to kill prey.

3. Larger soldier ants guard the ant troop

? This is a scorpion's sting. The scorpion swings the sting forward to inject poison into its prey.

Page 27

A troop of army ants marches across the forest floor. One group of the ants has attacked a much larger creature—a tiger beetle. A praying mantis munches on prey that it has seized with a lightning-fast movement of its front legs. Nearby, a tarantula and a centipede wait to catch insects running away from the ants.

5

6

4

Page 14

4 A praying mantis crushes its prey with strong jaws.

5 A tarantula waits for prey. It has a poisonous bite.

6 The centipede feeds on insects and spiders.

Locusts are a type of grasshopper and fly in huge groups called swarms. There may be billions of locusts in a swarm. The insects swoop down on farmers' fields and feed until there are no plants left.

Many **shield bugs** feed on plants. They have special mouthparts for piercing leaves and fruit and sucking up their juices. Shield bugs make a nasty smell if they are disturbed, so they're also called stinkbugs.

hawthorn shield bug

A leafcutter ant slices through a leaf with its strong jaws.

The ant takes the leaves back to its nest.

Plant eaters

More than half of all insects and creepy-crawlies are plant eaters. They feed on all parts of plants, including leaves, flowers, bark, and pollen. Some damage food crops, but others are helpful. They carry pollen between flowers so they are fertilized and can grow new plants.

Gardeners don't like **slugs** because they feed on the leaves of plants. Slugs are one of the worst garden pests.

slug

Boll weevils eat the buds of cotton plants. They do serious damage to the plants.

weevil piercing a cotton bud

Some plants fight back against greedy insects. **Sundew** leaves are covered with sticky drops that trap any insect that lands on them. The leaves then curl around the victim and eat it up.

This moth's wings beat so fast that they make a humming sound.

The sundew's hairlike leaves are tipped with beads of glue.

The hummingbird hawk moth has a very long tube for a mouth, like a drinking straw. It uses this to reach deep down into flowers and feed on the nectar inside.

1 The dragonfly catches its prey in flight.

2 Honeybees carry pollen from flower to flower.

3 A marbled white butterfly feeds on nectar.

What is this?

Page 30

Page 19

1

2

Fast fliers

Being able to fly gives insects a huge advantage over other creepy-crawlies. They can move around much more quickly than land-based creepy-crawlies. Flight allows insects to find food easily and to escape from their enemies. Most insects have two pairs of wings.

In a summer meadow, honeybees and hoverflies visit flowers to gather pollen and nectar, while butterflies perch on the flowers and sip the sweet nectar. Ladybugs fly from plant to plant hunting aphids. A speedy dragonfly zooms in searching for insect prey and startles a bush cricket.

Page 11

These are the tiny scales on a butterfly's wing that make its pretty patterns.

The caddis fly has hairs on its body as well as on its wings.

The hard front wings act as cases for the back wings.

A caddis fly looks a lot like a moth, but its wings are covered with tiny hairs instead of scales. (See its larva on page 17.)

a ladybug in flight

Like all beetles, a **ladybug** uses its fragile back wings for flying. The rest of the time, these wings are folded away, protected by the spotted front wings.

Special wings

Not all insect wings are the same. A beetle's front wings are very hard and protect the delicate back wings. Butterflies have two pairs of colorful, velvety wings, while flies have one pair of see-through wings. Wings aren't just for flying, either. Some insects use them to make sounds.

A bumblebee's wings beat at least 130 times per second.

Mosquito wings beat so fast that they make a whining noise.

Male crickets chirp to attract a mate. They make their song by rubbing their wings together. A scraper on one wing rubs against a ridge on the other wing.

A bumblebee makes a loud buzzing sound as it flies around. This is not the sound of its wings beating but of its flight muscles vibrating (shaking).

great green bush cricket

A crane fly has only one pair of wings.

Birdwing butterflies are the world's largest butterflies. The Cairns birdwing has an amazing wingspan of up to 6 in. (16cm)—yet it's only half the size of the record-breaking Queen Alexandra's birdwing!

Cairns birdwing

Knobbed stumps called halteres help the crane fly stay balanced.

Watch out!

Life is dangerous for insects and creepy-crawlies. They hunt one another, and there are always birds and other creatures ready to snap them up, too. But insects and creepy-crawlies have many ways to avoid danger and scare off enemies.

What is this?

1. A wasp can sting any attacker.

2. The stinkbug's bad smell puts off predators.

3. Ants bite or sting to attack and defend themselves.

? This is the eyespot on a caterpillar's behind. It makes the caterpillar look big and fierce.

Page 19

5

Page 30

6

Page 15

A colorful locust—
a type of grasshopper—
leaps up from the ground,
flashing its wings and startling
any predator. A stinkbug scares
off its enemy with a bad smell,
while a bombardier beetle squirts
boiling-hot chemicals at some
attacking ants. The ants are no
match for the beetle, even
though they can give a
painful sting.

3

4

4 The bombardier beetle sprays hot chemicals.

5 A locust can jump away from danger.

6 Foamy cuckoo spit protects a spittlebug's young.

Staying safe

To avoid being spotted, some insects and creepy-crawlies look like something else, such as a leaf or a thorn. Others are the same color as the flowers they live among. Some stay safe by disguising themselves as other, more dangerous, creatures.

The spider's legs are raised, ready to grab prey.

A praying mantis might be fierce, but it has enemies, too. Flower mantises are the same shape and color as the petals they usually perch on—which makes them very hard to spot.

Can you see the bush cricket on this lichen-covered tree trunk?

The mantis's red coloring is a perfect match for the flower.

crab spider on
a buttercup

wasp

Some insects **disguise themselves** as more dangerous insects. The hoverfly doesn't sting, but its striped body makes it look like a wasp or bee, which do sting. Thanks to this clever disguise, most predators steer clear of the hoverfly.

Crab spiders like to hide in flowers so they can ambush their prey. Some can even change color to match the flower they are on.

hoverfly

These strange-shaped **bugs** look just like thorns on a branch. As long as they stay still, birds and other insect eaters won't notice them.

This is the female thorn bug—she's a slightly different shape from the male.

Honeybees live almost all over the world and in almost every **habitat**. They build their nests in woodlands, fields, gardens, and tropical forests—anywhere that has flowers they can visit for food.

wild honeybee nest

Africa has hot, dry **grasslands** called savannas where few large trees grow. The savannas are home to billions of insects, including termites, ants, locusts, and grasshoppers.

Habitats

Milkweed plants contain poisonous, milky sap. Monarch caterpillars can eat the leaves without being harmed. They take in the poison, and this makes them taste bad to predators.

Many flowers contain **nectar**, a sweet liquid that insects like to eat. Insects come to the flowers to feed on nectar, and bees use nectar to make honey.

butterfly on a cistus flower

Plants

beekeeper

Honeybees are very useful insects. We love the honey they make for their food cells, and some people also eat pollen. Beeswax is used to make furniture polish and some candles.

bee on an apple blossom

There are **fewer and fewer bees**, and this could be a problem for farmers. Honeybees pollinate apples, carrots, and other food crops. Scientists think that pollution and pesticides might be harming bees.

Creepy-crawlies and us

Monarch butterflies make the **longest journeys** of any insect. They spend the winter in southern California or Mexico. In the spring, they fly as far as 2,500 mi. (4,000km) north to find the plants that their caterpillars like to eat.

Spittlebugs, or froghoppers, are **champion jumpers**, able to jump 100 times their own length. If you could do that, you could leap over your school!

spittlebug

Record breakers

More to explore

praying mantis

Tropical rainforests grow in parts of the world where it is hot and wet all year long. There are more types of insects and creepy-crawlies in rainforests than any other kind of animal.

Like all animals, insects need **water**. Most need water to drink. Some, such as mosquitoes and dragonflies, lay their eggs in water. The eggs hatch into swimming larvae that spend the first part of their lives in water.

mosquito eggs

Pollen looks like dust in the center of a flower. When an insect feeds on nectar, its body picks up pollen. Later, the pollen may brush off on another flower of the same kind, allowing that plant to produce seeds.

Water plants can live in water or float on the surface. They provide places for insects and creepy-crawlies to shelter, and they also shade the water.

water lily

Most insects and creepy-crawlies are harmless, but a few **bite and sting**. Some spiders have poisonous bites, while mosquitoes can suck our blood and spread deadly diseases.

Some insects are pests and **damage plants and crops**. Locusts are grasshoppers that sometimes form swarms. Hungry locusts can strip a farmer's fields in a single day.

desert locust

Dragonflies are **speedy** as well as beautiful. Large dragonflies can fly at an amazing 34 mph (55km/h) —that's faster than a car drives in a city.

Butterflies and moths have the **biggest wings** in the insect world. The atlas moth's wings are a whopping 12 in. (30cm) across.

atlas moth

Index